Teta's Wisdom
قالَتْ لي تيتا

Compiled by: Hiba El Chaarani
Illustrations and layout: Angela Nurpetlian

Published by Turning Point Books
15th Floor, Concorde Building, Dunan Street
Verdun, Beirut, Lebanon
P.O. Box: 14-6613
Tel: 00961 1 752 100
www.tpbooksonline.com

First edition: July 2010

Compiled by: Hiba El Chaarani
Illustrations and layout: Angela Nurpetlian

Text copyright © Turning Point, 2010
Layout and graphic design copyright © Turning Point, 2010
Illustration copyright © Angela Nurpetlian, 2010
Recipes copyright © Anissa Helou, 2010

Disclaimer: All information in this book is for informational purpose only and not to be taken as professional or expert advice. Pertaining to your specific health and body conditions, consult with a doctor or expert. We are not responsible for your use of information presented in this book.

All rights reserved.
No part of this publication may be reproduced or transmitted in any form or any means without the permission of the publisher.

ISBN: 978-9953-0-1799-0

Printing: **RAIDY**
www.raidy.com

Chapter 1
Home Sweet Home (p7)

Chapter 2
Family and Friends (p17)

Chapter 3
In the Kitchen (p29)

Chapter 4
Health and Wealth (p43)

Chapter 5
Words of Wisdom (p55)

This is a special year for Turning Point as we are celebrating our tenth anniversary. To mark this special occasion, we are launching *Teta's Wisdom*, a colorful and diverting title that shines a spotlight on one of Lebanon's most important family figures, the grandmother. Her priceless expressions, as well as her favorite recipes and some indispensable tips provide an important link with the past and deserve to be preserved for posterity. Turning Point is delighted to announce that 50% of the net sales from the book shall be donated to the Alzheimer's Association Lebanon (AAL), a charity that is committed to improving the lives of elderly people living with dementia.

We would like to thank all our partners: editors, illustrators, writers, graphic design artists, printers and book sellers who have worked with us over the past ten years and have contributed immeasurably to Turning Point's publishing vision. A special thank you to Marie-Joe Raidy, at Raidy Printing Group s.a.l., who has so kindly donated the cost of the pre-press and printing of this project.

Charlotte Hamaoui
Managing Director
Turning Point

A loved one's slow descent into Alzheimer is a shattering experience. "Alzheimer's Association Lebanon" (AAL) has brought hope to families and those they care for. Important knowledge developed internationally about Alzheimer's disease is offered in Lebanon through one-to-one counseling, support group meetings, a help line, monthly workshops and a very informative website. It also implements a broad program of public outreach and training workshops to change attitudes and misconceptions of professionals and society at large by de-stigmatizing Alzheimer's disease and creating awareness of its growing impact. AAL strives to change the experience into a joy of life. Only with your support and contribution can this important endeavor be sustained.

Diane Mansour
President
Alzheimer's Association Lebanon

البيت إلّي ربّاني ما بينساني.

The house that raised me does not forget me.

Chapter 1
Home Sweet Home
لا مكان كالمنزل

يلّي بدقّ الباب بيسمع الجواب.

The one who knocks on the door hears the answer.

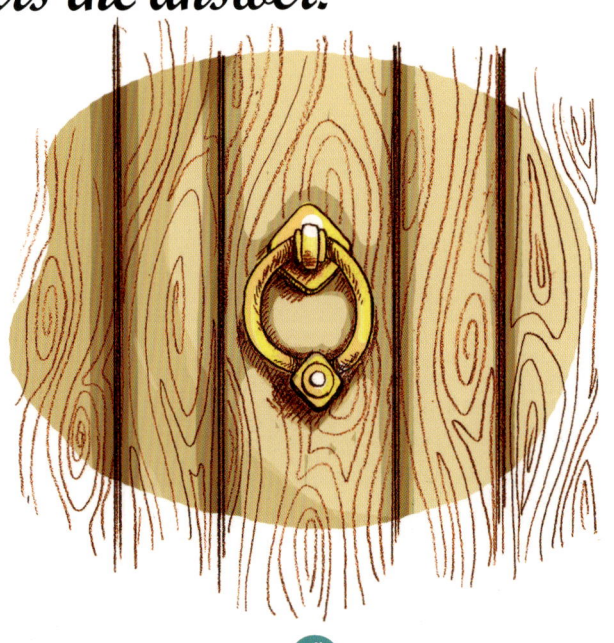

كلمة يا ريت ما بتعمّر بيت.

Regrets will not build houses.

Clean your face as you don't know who will kiss it and
clean your house as you don't know who will visit it.

غسّل وجهك ما بتعرف مين ببوسو
وغسّل بيتك ما بتعرف مين بدوسو.

Teta's Cleaning Tips

1) Soak clothes immediately in sugar and water and keep them overnight to remove fruit stains.

2) Clean the windows using newspapers with water and alcohol to obtain a clear surface.

3) Use soap flakes when cleaning the floor to obtain a brighter effect.

4) Sprinkle baby powder immediately on clothes to help remove oil stains.

5) To remove rust stains from cloth, rinse the item with water, add citric acid, then place it in the sunlight.

6) To remove lime scale from a kettle, put water and two tablespoons of citric acid for a short period of time.

7) In order to obtain clean and pure ice, boil the water first.

8) Use toothpaste before washing the item to remove ink stains from clothes.

9) If you want to avoid ironing your curtains, hang them immediately after washing them.

10) Remove chewing gum from clothes by directly putting the clothes in the freezer so that the gum hardens and is easily removed.

11) Soak clothes in aspirin and water to remove sweat stains.

إرشادات تيتا في عمليّة التنظيف:

1) انقع الملابس فوراً في الماء والسكّر، طوال اللّيل، لإزالة بُقع الفواكه عنها.
2) نظّف زجاج النّوافذ باستخدام الجرائد إضافة إلى الماء والسّبيرتو للحصول على سطح صافٍ.
3) إستخدِم برش الصّابون في الماء عند التّنظيف للحصول على أرضيّات أكثر لمعاناً.
4) رُشّ بودرة الأطفال فوراً على الملابس لإزالة بُقع الزيت عنها بسهولة.
5) إغسل القطعة الملوّثة بالصّدأ بالماء ثمّ رش عليها ملح اللّيمون وبعد ذلك ضعها تحت أشعّة الشّمس لإزالة الصّدأ عنها.
6) تخلّص من الطّبقة الكلسيّة في الغلّاية بإضافة ملعقتيْن من ملح اللّيمون إلى الماء الموجود فيها وبتركها منقوعةً في هذا السّائل لمدّة قصيرة.
7) إغلِ الماء أوّلاً للحصول على مكعبات ثلج نقيّة وخالية من الشوائب.
8) إستخدم معجون الأسنان فوراً لإزالة بُقع الحبر عن الملابس.
9) علّق السّتائر مباشرةً بعد غسلها، وذلك لتجنّب كيّها.
10) أزل العلكة عن الملابس بوضعها فوراً في الثّلاجة حتى تقسو ويسهُل نزعها.
11) انقع الملابس في الماء والأسبرين لإزالة بُقع العرق عنها.

بواب مغلقة وهموم مفرقة.
You don't know what goes on behind closed doors.

لو في خير ما رماه الطّير.

If there were good in it, then the bird wouldn't have thrown it away.

يلّي بيتو من قزاز ما يراشق العالم بالحجارة.

People who live in glass houses shouldn't throw stones.

Chapter 2
Family and Friends
العائلة والأصدقاء

رجعت حليمة لعادتها القديمة.

Halima always goes back to her old habits.

ذكور الدّيب وهيّ القضيب.

Speak of the devil.

كلّ عرس إلو قرص.
Every wedding has a hitch.

طنجرة ولاقت غطاها.
A pot found its lid.

بيعمل من الحبّة قبّة.
He turns a seed into a dome.
(He makes a mountain out of a mole-hill).

خدو البنات من صدور العمّات.

A girl takes after her paternal aunt.

خود أسرارهن من صغارهن.

Learn their secrets from their children.

أنا وخيّي على إبن عمّي وأنا وإبن عمّي على الغريب.

My brother and I against my cousin,
my cousin and I against the stranger.

Teta's Sleeping Tips

1) Wake up and go to bed at the same time every day.
2) Read to relax directly before going to bed.
3) Keep the room at a moderate temperature.
4) Keep the lights dim.
5) Keep a time period of three to four hours between eating and going to bed. Take a very small snack before sleeping if you are hungry.
6) Avoid caffeinated drinks (tea, coffee…) three hours before sleeping. Instead, take a cup of anis seed tea (yansoon).
7) Eat apples and lettuce, they are known for their good sleeping effect.
8) Take a warm bath before going to bed, as it relaxes the body and sets you to sleep.
9) Drink warm milk or yoghurt before sleeping.

إرشادات تيتا لنوم عميق ومريح:

1) حافظ على وقتٍ محدّدٍ للإستيقاظ وللنّوم كلّ يوم.
2) إقرأ للإسترخاء مباشرةً قبل النّوم.
3) أبقِ حرارة الغرفة معتدلة.
4) أبقِ الأضواء خافتة.
5) اجعل المدّة بين تناول الطّعام والخلود إلى النّوم من ثلاث إلى أربع ساعات. وإذا شعرت بالجوع، تناول وجبة خفيفة جداً قبل النّوم.
6) تجنّب تناول الكافيين (الشّاي، والقهوة...) قبل النّوم بثلاث ساعات وحاول إستبدالها بشراب اليانسون.
7) تناول التفّاح و الخسّ، فمن المعروف أنّ أثرهما جيّد في عمليّة النّوم.
8) خُذ حماماً دافئاً قبل النّوم، فهو يُخفّف من توتّر الجسم، ويساعد في النّوم.
9) اشرَب الحليب الدّافئ أو اللّبن قبل النّوم.

قلبي على إبني وقلب إبني على الحجر.

My heart is with my son, but my son's heart is as hard as stone.

حظو من السّما إلّي بتحبّو الحمى.

He whose mother-in-law loves him is such a lucky man.

يلّي بشوفني بعين بشوفو بعينتين.
He who sees me with one eye,
I see him with two.

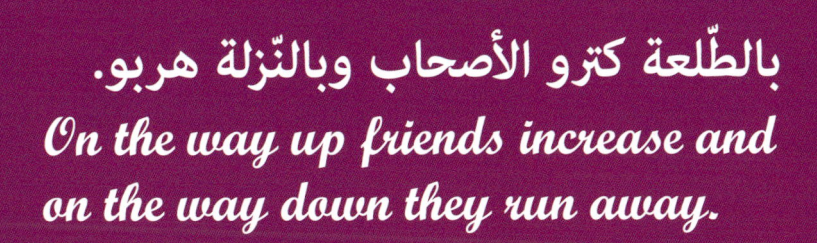

بالطّلعة كترو الأصحاب وبالنّزلة هربو.
On the way up friends increase and on the way down they run away.

قاضي الأولاد شنق حالو.
A children's judge will hang himself.

حترنا يا قرعة من وين نبوسك.
You confused us, you bald head, about where we should kiss you!
(Whatever I do, you're never satisfied).

الرجّال رحمة لو بالبيت فحمة.

A man in the house is valuable even if he's a piece of coal.

الولد ولد، ولو حكم بلد.

A child will be a child, even if he is running a country.

كول على زوقك ولبوس على زوق الناس.

*Eat according to your taste,
but dress according to others'.*

Chapter 3
In the Kitchen
في المطبخ

Teta's Lemonada
Lemonade

Makes 1 liter

Juice of 4 lemons
4 tablespoons sugar, or to taste

Pour the lemon juice into a large pitcher. Add 3-4 cups water depending on how sour you like your lemonade and stir in the sugar.

Dissolve the sugar completely before adding ice cubes. Taste and adjust the sweetness if necessary and serve immediately.

Optional: add mint leaves.

Teta's Murabbah el-Mishmosh
Apricot Jam

Makes three 500g jars

1kg fresh halved apricots
with seed removed
750g granulated sugar

Put the apricots and sugar in a saucepan. Place over medium heat and bring to boil. Reduce the heat and boil for 15-20 minutes, stirring regularly, or until the sugar syrup has thickened and the apricot halves have softened.

Remove from the heat and let cool. Fill sterilized jars with the jam, cover with waxed paper, close the jars and store at room temperature.

Teta's Ghraybeh
White Shortbread Biscuits

Makes 36 pieces

100g unsalted butter, softened
125g icing sugar
2 tablespoons orange-blossom water (maazahr)
2 tablespoons rose water (maawared)
250g fine semolina
50g raw pistachio nuts (optional)

Preheat the oven to 170°C.
Blend the softened butter and icing sugar in a mixing bowl with the back of a wooden spoon until you have a creamy, smooth white paste.
Work in the flour gradually until it is fully incorporated, then add the orange-blossom and rose water and knead with your hand until the dough is soft and smooth. Refrigerate for about 1 hour.
Pinch off a piece of dough the size of a walnut and roll it into a sausage shape - about 1.5cm thick and 10cm long.

Bring both ends together, slightly overlapping them, to shape a ring. Flatten the ring a little. Press a pistachio nut where the ends join and place on a non-stick baking sheet. Continue shaping and garnishing the ghraybeh until you have finished the pastry and the nuts.

Bake for 15 minutes or until the dough is cooked but still white. Transfer to a metal grill. Let cool completely before transferring to a serving platter or an airtight biscuit container.

You can shape ghraybeh in different ways, either in round cakes about 5cm in diameter and 2cm thick, with a slightly depressed center in which you press an almond or a pistachio nut, or in diamonds the same thickness as before and with sides about 5cm long, also with a central nut garnish.

كول توم وإنسى الهموم.
Eat garlic and forget your worries.

كول بصل وإنسى إلّي حصل.
Eat onions and forget the past.

ما كلّ مين صفّ صواني قال أنا حلواني.

Not anyone who arranges trays can claim he's the sweet maker.

Teta's Meghli
Caraway and Cinnamon Custard

You can buy ready-made meghli mixture that is a quick alternative to the home made one.

Serves 4

2.5L water
100g ground rice
2 ½ tablespoons ground caraway seeds
1 ½ tablespoons ground anis
1 ½ teaspoons ground cinnamon
200g golden caster sugar
dried coconut for garnish
60g pine nuts, soaked in boiling water
60g walnuts, soaked in boiling water then peeled
60g blanched almond halves, soaked in boiling water

Put the rice in a large saucepan. Add the water, ground caraway seeds and anis and place over a high heat. Bring to boil while stirring constantly. Keep stirring for 25 minutes. Then reduce the heat to medium and boil for another 5 minutes, still stirring. Add the cinnamon and stir for another 20 minutes, then reduce the heat to medium-low, add the sugar and stir for 10 more minutes.

Take the pan off the heat and pour the mixture into one shallow serving bowl or into 4 or 6 individual ones depending on their sizes. Leave to cool, then garnish with the shredded coconut and drained nuts and serve chilled or at room temperature.

Teta's Kitchen Tips

1) When boiling eggs, add salt to the water so eggs boil faster and the shells don't crack.
2) Apply cold water and two spoons of salt so frozen chicken defrosts faster.
3) Boil vegetables after adding both sugar and salt to the water to maintain the fresh green color.
4) Preserve the good taste of olive oil by storing it in a dark place, preferably wrapped in a paper bag or cloth.
5) Use bay leaves while cooking chicken to diminish the smell.
6) When boiling beans, add oil to the water to avoid froth from spilling.
7) When preparing a salad, add salt at the end just before serving to keep the vegetables fresh.
8) Store turnip pickles in a dark area to maintain their bright red color.
9) Do not store bananas in the fridge, otherwise they will turn black.
10) When preparing cakes, cover the pan with sesame paste (tahina) so that the batter doesn't stick after baking.
11) When preparing dough, add sugar to the yeast to speed up the yeast's effect.

إرشادات تيتا في المطبخ:

1) أضف الملح إلى الماء لتسريع عمليّة سلق البيض، ولتجنّب تكسّر قشره.
2) ضع الدّجاج المثلّج في ماء بارد مع ملعقتين من الملح وذلك لإذابته سريعاً.
3) أسلُق الخضار بعد إضافة السّكر والملح إلى الماء للحفاظ على لونها الأخضر النضر.
4) حافظ على جودة طعم زيت الزّيتون بتخزينه في مكانٍ معتم، ويُفضّل أن يوضع في كيسٍ من الورق أو القماش.
5) إستعمل ورق الغار لتجنُّب رائحة الدّجاج الكريهة في أثناء طبخه.
6) أضف القليل من الزيت إلى الماء لتجنّب انسكاب الرغوة عند سلق الحبوب.
7) أضف الملح إلى السّلطة مباشرةً قبل تقديمها، وذلك لإبقاء الخضار طازجة.
8) خزّن اللّفت المخلّل في مكانٍ معتم للحفاظ على لونه الأحمر الزّاهي.
9) لا تضع الموز في البرّاد وإلا أصبح لونه أسود.
10) ادهَن الصّينية بالطّحينة عند تحضير قوالب الكاتو كي لا يلتصق الخليط بالقعر خلال الخَبز.
11) أضف السّكر إلى الخميرة عند صنع العجينة لتسريع عمليّة التّخمير.

Teta's Sfoof
Yellow Cakes

Serves 10

3 tablespoons milk powder
500g fine semolina (firkha flour)
250g plain white flour
2 tablespoons turmeric
1 ½ tablespoons baking powder
200g unsalted butter or 200ml vegetable oil
500g golden caster sugar
400ml warm water
30g pine nuts or blanched almonds for garnish

Preheat the oven to 180°C and grease a deep baking dish with a tablespoon of tahinah. Put the milk powder, fine semolina, flour, turmeric and baking powder in a large bowl and mix well.

In another mixing bowl, add the sugar and the butter (or the oil) to the warm water and stir until well blended. Add this mixture to the flour and semolina and blend together. Pour the mixture into the baking dish and scatter the pine nuts or almonds on top. Bake for 35 minutes or until the cake has risen and is cooked from the inside.

Remove from the oven, leave to cool, then cut into medium squares or diamonds and serve at room temperature. These cakes will keep for a week if stored in a sealed container and kept in a cool place.

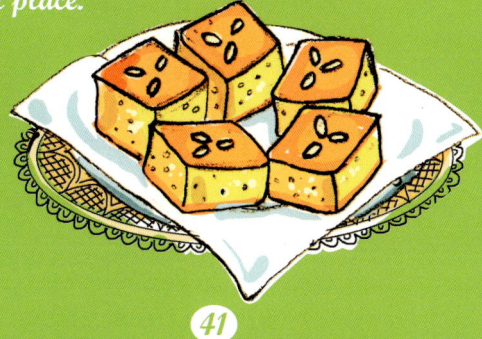

خبّي قرشك الأبيض ليومك الأسود.

Hide your white penny for your black day.

Chapter 4
Health and Wealth
الصّحّة والرّخاء

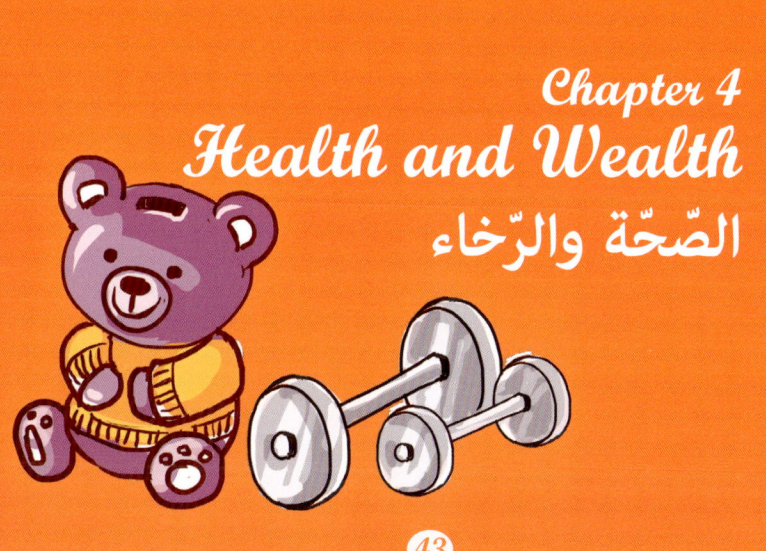

المال فدى الأبدان.

Your health is worth your wealth.

نام بكّير وفيق بكّير وشوف الصحّة كيف بتصير.

Sleep early, wake early, and notice how your health will improve.

Teta's Body Care Tips

1) Remove chicken or fish smell by rubbing your hands with half a lemon or a lettuce leaf.
2) Get rid of dandruff and make your hair shinier by rinsing with vinegar.
3) Get rid of bad breath by eating parsley or mint.
4) Moisturize and purify skin by placing cucumber slices on your face.
5) Relieve itching from a mosquito bite by rinsing it with water and salt.
6) Treat a bee sting by rubbing your skin with a slice of fresh garlic.

إرشادات تيتا للعناية بالجسم:

1) أزِل رائحة الدَّجاج أو السَّمك بفرك يديك بنصف قطعة من اللّيمون الحامض أو بورقةِ خسٍّ.
2) تخلَّص من قشرة الرّأس واجعل شعرك أكثر لمعاناً بغسله بقليلٍ من الخلِّ.
3) تخلَّص من رائحة الفم الكريهة بمضغ عرقٍ من البقدونس أو النّعناع.
4) رطِّبْ البشرة ونقِّها بوضع شرائح من الخيار على وجهك.
5) خَفِّفْ من الحكّة النّاتجة من لدغة البعوض بغسلها بالماء والملح.
6) عالِج لسعة النّحلة بفرك جلدك بالثّوم الطّازج.

المال بجرّ المال والقمل بجرّ السّيبان.

Money leads to money and lice lead to lice.

على قدّ بساطك مدّ إجريك.
Do not stretch your legs longer than your mat.

سآل مجرّب ولا تسأل حكيم.

Instead of consulting a doctor, take the advice of the experienced.

بيضة اليوم أحسن من ديك بكرا.

Today's egg is better than tomorrow's rooster.

Teta's Home Remedies

1) Soothe sore tonsils by gargling twice per day with tea at room temperature.
2) Lighten tummy aches by drinking chamomile tea and rubbing your tummy with alcohol.
3) Fight a cold by soaking your feet in hot water and salt.
4) Treat back aches by massaging your back with hot olive oil.
5) Bring down a fever by placing a cloth dabbed with vinegar on your forehead.
6) Fight constipation by drinking carob molasses (dibs) diluted in hot water.
7) Treat a cough by taking a spoon of sesame paste (tahina).
8) Treat indigestion by taking two spoons of orange-blossom water (maazahr) diluted in hot water.
9) Treat diarrhea and vomiting by avoiding all food and eating yoghurt, rice, boiled potatoes and toast. A few sips of 7-Up also help.
10) Treat dizziness by drinking a glass of water with sugar and a teaspoon of orange-blossom water (maazahr).
11) Treat menstrual pain and stomach pain by drinking boiled mint.
12) Relieve rashes or skin allergies by washing them with rose water (maawared).

وصفات تيتا العلاجيّة:

1) داوِ احتقان اللّوزتين بالغرغرة بالشّاي الفاتر مرّتين في اليوم.
2) خفِّف من آلام بطنك بشُرب البابونج وبدعكه بالسّبيرتو.
3) قاوِم الزّكام بنقع رجليك في الماء الدّافئ والملح.
4) عالِج آلام الظّهر بتدليك ظهرك بزيت الزّيتون السّاخن.
5) خفِّض حِدّة الحُمّى بوضع قطعة قماش مبلّلة بالقليل من الخلّ على جبينك.
6) عالِج الإمساك بشُرب دبس الخرّوب المخفَّف بالماء السّاخن.
7) عالِج السُّعال بتناول ملعقة من الطّحينة.
8) عالِج عُسَر الهضم بتناول ملعقتين من ماء الزّهر الممزوج بالماء السّاخن.
9) عالِج الإسهال والتّقيّؤ بتجنّب كافّة المأكولات. وبتناوُل اللّبن والأرزّ والبطاط المسلوقة والخبز المحمّص. كما أنّ القليل من مشروب السّفن أب يفيد أيضاً.
10) داوِ الدّوّار بشُرب كوب من الماء المحلّى بالسّكّر مع ملعقة صغيرة من ماء الزّهر.
11) داوي آلام الحيض والبطن بشُرب النّعناع المغليّ.
12) خفِّف من تورّم الطّفح الجلديّ أو الحساسيّة بغسل الجسم بماء الورد.

الأعور بمملكة العميان ملك.

The one-eyed man is a king in the country of the blind.

Chapter 5
Words of Wisdom
أقوال وحِكم

إذا كان الحكي من فضّة فالسّكوت من ذهب.

If speaking is of silver, then silence is of gold.

لو بدها تشتّي كانت غيّمت.

*If it were going to rain,
it would have clouded.*

Seasons

أيلول طرفو بالشّتي مبلول.
The end of September is soaked with rain.

بتمّوز الميّ بتغلي بالكوز.
In July, the water boils in the jug.

برد تشرين بخزّأ المصارين.
November's cold tears through the intestines.

خبّي فحماتك الكبار لآذار الغدّار.
Save your big coals,
for March the backstabber.

حبل الكذب قصير.
The life of a lie is short.

الفاضي بيعمل قاضي.
The idle man becomes a judge.

علّمناهن على الشّحادة سبقونا على البواب.

We taught them how to beg,
they beat us to the doors.

الجمل لو شاف حردبتو كان وقع وفكّ رقبتو.

If a camel could see its hump,
it would fall and break its neck.

(If one could see his flaws, he would be shocked).

غاب القطّ إلعب يا فار.

When the cat is away,
the mice will play.

عصفور بالإيد ولا عشرة على الشجرة.

A bird in the hand is better than ten on the tree.